With the new day comes
new strength and new thoughts.

—ELEANOR ROOSEVELT

Every day is a new beginning.
Treat it that way. Stay away from what might
have been, and look at what can be.

—MARSHA PETRIE SUE

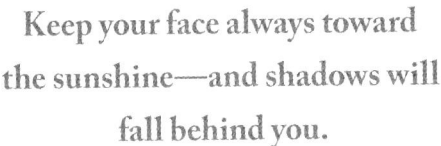

Keep your face always toward
the sunshine—and shadows will
fall behind you.

—WALT WHITMAN

I hope you realize that every day is a fresh start
for you. That every sunrise is a new chapter in
your life waiting to be written.

—JUANSEN DIZON,
CONFESSIONS OF A WALLFLOWER

Each day provides its own gifts.

—Marcus Aurelius

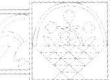

The next morning dawned bright and sweet,
like ribbon candy.

—SARAH ADDISON ALLEN,
GARDEN SPELLS

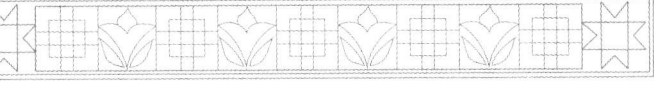

With this morning's sunrise comes a day
of things that have never been.

—Toni Sorenson

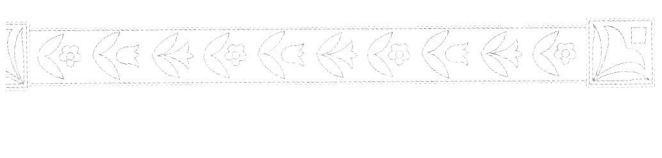

...rise full of eagerness and energy, knowing well
what achievement lies ahead of me.

—ZANE GREY